The Fat, Lazy American

How to Make a
Total Transformation of Your Life,
Make It Last For the Rest of Your Life
and Why You Should Do It NOW

Dr. David Robinson

ISBN 0-7414-3360-5

Revised 2004, Formerly: Be Healthy Be Happy Be Fit Live Smart, ©2002

Robinson, David/The Fat, Lazy American/How to Make a Total Transformation of Your Life, Make It Last for the Rest of Your Life and Why You Should Do it NOW

1. Self help
2. Health
3. Fitness
4. Nutrition
5. Spiritual

Published by:

INFINITY PUBLISHING.COM

1094 New DeHaven Street, Suite 100
West Conshohocken, PA 19428-2713
Info@buybooksontheweb.com
www.buybooksontheweb.com
Toll-free (877) BUY BOOK
Local Phone (610) 941-9999
Fax (610) 941-9959

Printed in the United States of America

Printed on Recycled Paper

Published November 2006

Contents

"You are what you think about all day long"

Henry David Thoreau

Disclaimer

This book is not intended to be a substitute for professional health care from a licensed health care provider.

This is a self-help guide and not a quick-fix for weight loss or physical body changes.

Anyone who decides to enhance or change any aspect of their lifestyle for the better on a permanent basis must expect to invest time and effort.

This book should be used only as a guide.

The purpose of this manual is as a reference for enhancing individual health and establishing necessary health coverage.

The author shall have neither liability nor responsibility to any person or entity with respect to any loss or damage caused, or alleged to have caused, directly or indirectly, by the information contained in this guide.

Acknowledgments

My sincere and heartfelt gratitude to all those who assisted me in bringing this book to fruition.

To my parents for their unending support.

Special thanks to all those folks in the fitness centers, from Boston to San Diego, that I have had the pleasure of working with and working-out at.

To the many people whose wisdom was gleaned in making publishing this guide an attainable goal.

But especially to *you*, the reader, for having the courage, conviction and strength of fortitude to step out of your comfort zone and use this book to begin evolving a life of better living and of reaching toward better health.

To the Source, for the gift of good health and life.

About the Author

Dr. Robinson received his B.S. in biology at Bridgewater State College in Massachusetts and his D.C. from Life University, College of Chiropractic in Atlanta.

After 7 years in a full time practice as a chiropractor, he received his fitness certifications as a Personal Trainer, Fitness Counselor, and Aerobic Instructor from the Aerobics and Fitness Association of America, Los Angeles.

David then divided his time for the next 7 years between a part-time practice and Fitness Training and Counseling part time.

He has been a trainer for one of the 12-week Police Cadet Training Programs of the Massachusetts Criminal Justice Training Council, as well as working in fitness centers on Massachusetts' South Shore and in San Diego.

For over 25 years, Dr. Robinson has maintained great health through living a healthy lifestyle as outlined in this guide.

David lives and works on the South Coast of Massachusetts.

A Note to the Reader

For the majority of you, YOU are the main aggressor against your own health. YOU constantly attack it every minute of your life via your poor lifestyle and habit-patterns. Your health is *not* good and any single event can take hold of your defenses, overcome them, and take you down to chronic illness, fast!

My passion for helping people to become more aware of a healthier way of life and achieve a higher level of health, and protect that health, lies within these pages.

Today's working people have schedules that our grandparents would be alarmed at. The time pressure is intense. Being aware of this, I have written this condensed guide so that it may be read and absorbed easily and quickly.

This book is a *comprehensive reference guide to lasting heath & health care*, to learning how to acquire total good health, body, mind, and spirit and establish health coverage *tailored to your needs.* A guide for changing your life toward great health and longevity *is in your hands!*

Given the current trend of "play-or-pay" mandatory health insurance as started in Massachusetts, this guide is indispensable. Especially when the very real possibility exists that our health care industry may take the same road.

As the advertisement many years ago said, *when you've got your health, you've got just about everything!* This guide teaches you "about everything" to get good health. I hope you enjoy and value this guide to enhancing your life in all aspects every day of your life.

Namaste,
David

"I conjecture that of the vast majority of Americans who fall into the category of the title of this book, less than ½ of 1% of them have the courage, the conviction, the fortitude to establish & maintain fit, healthy lifestyle habit-patterns. This *MUST* change!"

Dr. David W. Robinson

PART I

WHY You Should Do It *NOW*

1

Americans in Health Crisis

Dorland's Medical Dictionary: HEALTH: a state of physical, mental and social well-being. *Holistic:* a system of preventive medicine that takes into account the whole individual, his own responsibility for his well-being, and the total influences – social, psychological, environmental – that affect health, including nutrition, exercise, and mental relaxation. *Public:* the field of medicine concerned with safeguarding and improving the health of the community as a whole.

Definitions from an accepted medical source cast light on the fact that health encompasses a much broader scope than most people care to admit to. It is far easier for people to stick their heads in the sand and make excuses as to why they participate in unhealthy rituals; rituals, because they are continually indulged in, by choice.

Health encompasses all those things that are regularly heard about. Exercise, proper nutrition and supplementation, rest and relaxation, spiritual practices, etc. But it also includes 'activities of daily living' and the manner in which they are conducted.

A good percentage of Americans are involved in some very disturbing lifestyle habit-patterns.

Frequent and recurring episodes of: overeating, eating high fat, high sugar foods and fast foods daily, not exercising the prescribed minimum, smoking, abusing alcohol, over-the-counter and prescription drugs, speeding, aggressive driving, not wearing a seat belt, running red lights and stop signs, listening to deafeningly loud music with earphones, a rushed, high stress, lack of relaxation/meditation daily schedule.

Bottom line for the average American's lifestyle? Unhealthy as hell. The statistics prove it. The statistics, often reported separately and infrequently, when brought together, breach alarming.

- The US Surgeon General reports that approximately 45% of US adults use tobacco regularly and about 65% of Americans are overweight to obese.
- Less than 15% of US adults exercise 60 minutes or more a minimum of 3 times each week.
- A recent report on National Public Radio cited the Centers for Disease Control's report that about 13% of US children ages 8 – 16 are overweight to obese.
- Almost half of teens ages 13 – 19 smoke.
- Less than 10% of kids ages 8 – 18 exercise for 60 minutes or more 3 times week.

To include statistics on death and injury from accidents involving speeding, running red lights and stop signs, aggressive driving and DUI, use of illegal drugs and abuse of prescription drugs and alcohol, would have this information approach macabre.

These statistics are why health insurance premiums and health care fees are high and climbing higher.

Needless to say, the majority of Americans continue to do the things that make them fat and sick and injure or harm their bodies, and continue to avoid the activities that are healthy and can prevent illness or injury.

It appears, at least from the statistics previously cited, that sloth, gluttony, and irresponsible behavior are the favored lifestyle habit-patterns.

The problem is that these choices are stretching and straining the conventional medical care establishment and health insurance industry in this country to its limits.

Frequent and recurring crisis care, resulting from frequent and recurring illness and injury, as a result of continual poor choices (sloth and gluttony and irresponsible actions) has proven to be extraordinarily expensive and getting more expensive.

The Centers for Disease Control in Atlanta have cited the costs for this.

- More than 300,000 people die each year from illnesses caused by or made worse by obesity.
- More than 430,000 die each year from smoking related illnesses.
- The UCLA RAND Center found that obesity raises a person's health care costs by 36% and medication costs by 77% (an average $395 per year), while these people have 30% – 50% more chronic medical problems.
- It also found that smoking leads to a 21% rise in health care costs and 28% rise in medication costs (an average $230 per year).
- According to the Centers for Medicare and Medicaid Services, US spending for health care will top 3 trillion by 2010.
- ***57% of all illness & injury is a result of lifestyle*** – BlueCross BlueShield of Mass.

The following *World Health Organization* statistics are less than surprising with this in mind.

- *U.S. citizens ranked 37 among 191 nations in ability to improve health*

- *Over 15% of U.S. Gross Domestic Product is spent on correcting health problems*
- *Over 72% of all deaths in U.S. are the result of heart disease, lung disease, diabetes & degenerative diseases*

In July of 2000, WHO released statements that less than 10% of the media (print, radio, TV) carried.

- *The very expensive U.S. drug-based system is NOT reducing the rate at which conditions become chronic and continue to plague the U.S.*
- *Such conditions are preventable for the most part and are primarily resulting from unhealthy practices*

One year later, WHO spoke out again.

- *Medical care in the U.S. has its place, but it is not providing the answers needed to improve health and quality of life.*

The state of health, the daily habit-patterns, health behaviors and lifestyles of most Americans that lead to the above statistics are, quite obviously, pathetic.

This population continues to show apathy toward gaining and maintaining good health and fitness.

Beyond this, they continue to display and express a negative arrogance toward healthy lifestyles and habit-patterns.

How, in light of statistics like these, can insurance companies not be justified in continuing to increase premiums and decrease coverage each year?

It makes sense, in order to minimize losses against a public continually engaging in behaviors that make them sick and unhealthy; thus resulting in over-utilizing the health care system and insurance policies.

How can Americans really expect changes in the health care and health insurance industries outside of these double-digit % increases in fees and premiums every year? Based on these statistics, most Americans deserve higher premiums and fees.

The majority of people in this country value, have the time for, have the money for, have the insatiable desire for the new styles, the new truck or SUV, the movies, the football and baseball and basketball and hockey games, the entertainment each weekend, the new furniture, the manicure, the hair style, the new gadget or toy, the vacations, the lottery tickets, the casino, the lunches and dinners out all week, anything that makes them 'look good' and 'look stylish' to others, anything that makes them 'feel good' physically or emotionally, for that fix of immediate gratification.

But when it comes to spending time, effort, and money on joining a fitness center, working out regularly, following the *Food Pyramid*, buying and taking nutritional supplements, relaxation/meditation time daily, learning about and seeking out preventive health care practices and routines, and maintaining good health, the only thing people always have are excuses why they *can't* or *don't*.

These statistics prove that most Americans simply *refuse, by choice,* to place any value on healthy lifestyles and conduct themselves in a manner that is congruent with the *Dorland's Medical Dictionary* definitions of *health*.

The most recent statistic, released in October of 2002, is that over 42 million American citizens are without any health insurance.

Combine that with the most recent statistic from BlueCross

BlueShield of Massachusetts; that over 57% of all illnesses and injuries are directly related to lifestyle, and you have a double-edged crisis.

All the efforts to coax people into healthier lifestyles and all the legislation and programs to change the health delivery system for the better have failed and are still failing.

Add these factors together and you get the necessity for drastic changes. Drastic change *is* imperative. Drastic change *is* a matter of *when*; not *if*.

Just look again at the previous statistics. Understand a system that is trillions of dollars in debt, and then accept the coming reality of a *Brave New World* of mandatory merit-rated health insurance for all citizens and of lifestyle tracking & profiling.

It has already begun in the state of Massachusetts! Mandatory health insurance is being legislated as this book is being written!

Americans have been grossly negligent about their own health and lifestyles. They have refused to acknowledge that, first and foremost, health begins with self. That health is primarily *their own*, an individual responsibility.

Such irresponsible lifestyles have proved extraordinarily costly to health insurers, health care institutions, and the government.

As a result, those changes have already begun!

2

The *Novus Ordo* of Health Insurance

When constant entertainment, gluttony, and sloth take priority over maintaining good health, then face it and accept it: the American public's value system is warped.

Look at the realities: two 40-year-old males in the same city purchase the same health insurance policy from the same health insurance company.

Male #1 is fit, a non-smoker, has a strength & aerobic training fitness routine 4-5 times a week, eats according to the *Food Pyramid* and all other nutritional recommendations, takes proper supplements, is rarely ill, meditates daily, sees a chiropractor and massage therapist once a month, does not speed or drive aggressively, and, in general, leads a responsible, healthy lifestyle. He represents approximately 9% of the population.

Male #2 is obese, does not work out at all, smokes a pack a day, eats primarily according to the *Food Pyramid* upside-down, doesn't see a chiropractor or massage therapist, speeds excessively and drives aggressively, is stressed and rushed and sick 2-3 times each year, and, in general, has a poor lifestyle with poor habit-patterns. He represents approximately 67% of the population.

But both males pay similar premiums!

That's *unjustified* and has been for decades. And, it all may have to very well end.

Those who lead healthy lives and follow a healthy lifestyle should not be paying the same premiums for the same health insurance policies as those who lead unhealthy and irresponsible lifestyles.

That said, the state of health, the daily habit-patterns, health behaviors and lifestyles of most Americans are deplorable.

Further, the U.S. population continues to show apathy toward gaining and maintaining good health and fitness.

Beyond this, they continue to display and express a negative arrogance toward healthy lifestyles and habit-patterns.

Dramatic change has become *imperative*.

If the unhealthy majority doesn't begin to value healthy living, it is likely that they will end up literally paying for their sloth, gluttony, and irresponsibility.

The time will come when the burden of paying for those unhealthy lifestyles is squarely on the shoulders of those who continue to engage in them.

The system can no longer fiscally tolerate spreading the burden of the unhealthy majority, who over-utilize the system, by leveling the same premiums and fees upon those who make the daily effort to maintain healthy, fit, and responsible lifestyle habit-patterns and rarely use the system.

Mandatory Minimum Merit-Rated Health Insurance & Lifestyle Contributed Surcharges sound extremely familiar when looking at the automobile and home insurance industries.

Leading a responsible and healthy lifestyle should result in the benefit of prorated (lower) premiums. Leading an unhealthy lifestyle should result in paying greater premiums each year.

Those who crunch the numbers and statistics in the health

care system know that this is a way to reduce premiums and costs across the board.

Let's take a look at how it may all come about.

Forming 3MRHI & LCS

The federal government and Health Care Finance Administration (HCFA) establish coverage parameters and legislation for *Mandatory Minimum Merit-Rated Health Insurance* for all citizens.

A Mandatory Minimum amount of Health Insurance Coverage is established that all citizens <u>must</u> carry. Coverage above and beyond this minimum would be offered by insurers at increased premiums.

A *Base Premium* for this *MMHIC* is calculated and formulated for each geographic-economic area in the same manner as the BC/BS Association presently utilizes to determine its Premiums.

All health insurers would be mandated to provide *3MRHI*

The current health care insurers gradually place all citizens onto the system within 3 years of passage of legislation instituting *3MRHI.*

The current health care insurance system is gradually replaced by placing all citizens new-born to 19 years of age onto the system within 1 year of passage of legislation; all citizens 20–60 years of age onto the system the following year; all citizens 61+ onto the system the next year.

Upon becoming a member of the *3MRHI* system, each individual would be issued a *3MRHI* card.

The Health Care Finance Administration (HCFA) would

utilize the central data collection center, *Collosus,* for *3MRHI.*

All pharmacies, fitness clubs, health care offices & institutions, and insurers would be linked up with this central system.

An individual's *3MRHI* card is scanned/swiped for *every* drug, tobacco, alcohol purchase, when entering & exiting fitness centers and when utilizing health care providers/ institutions.

Collected data from all above sources would be sent to this data collection center, *Collosus*.

All such purchases, uses, utilizations, activities in this system would be assigned a *Health Value*; a numeric value from 0 (unhealthy) to 10 (extremely healthy).

The system would calculate, on a monthly basis, the average *Health Value* from each individual's data to determine their overall yearly *Lifestyle Index* from 0 (unhealthy) to 10 (extremely healthy), by averaging the monthly *Health Values*.

Each individual's annual premium for the *3MRHI* would be based on this *Lifestyle Index.*

A "Base Premium" would be set at a *Lifestyle Index* of level 5.

An individual's *3MRHI* annual premium would be surcharged (increased) a set dollar amount for each *Lifestyle Index* level below 5.

An individual's *3MRHI* would be credited (decreased) a set dollar amount for each *LI* level above 5.

These premiums, less any surcharges, but including all

credits, would be fully tax deductible.

Under the *3MRHI* and *LI* system, each person would be subject to a *Lifestyle Contributed Surcharge* due at each utilization of any health care provider.

An individual's *LI* value (0 to 10) would determine the amount of the *Lifestyle Contributed Surcharge* (now called "co-payment") due at each utilization of any health care provider/service.

This is a merit-rated health insurance system, much like many states' auto insurance system. If we can merit-rate our behavior behind a wheel, then we can merit-rate our behavior in activities of daily living and our lifestyle habit-patterns.

Regulating Health Care Costs

The present-day geographic-economic methodology, utilized by the BlueCross BlueShield Association of insurers to cap what is paid to providers for services, pharmaceuticals, medical equipment, etc., would be utilized in the same manner under the *3MRHI* system.

Patients would only be responsible for the *LCS* payments to providers or institutions beyond what the *3MRHI* system payment is for the service, etc. The *LCS* would be the replacement for present day co-payments and deductibles.

Regulating Malpractice Litigations

The injured party would be given two options.

The first would be in the form of a monetary reward to plaintiffs and would be capped at $1M. The second option would be an award for a set period of time of gratis care, and waived *3MRHI* premiums not to exceed the period of determined *maximum medical improvement* of the injury or up to a 3 year maximum.

Regulating Malpractice Insurance Premiums

Malpractice insurers would be required to form a "pool," much like states do for home-owners insurance along coastal areas. In order to spread the cost of liability payments, each insurer would be required to pay an equal amount toward such a payment.

Malpractice premiums would be calculated in a similar fashion as these insurers presently calculate rates.

Surcharges and *Credits* would be applied to the base premiums only for number-of-claims and number-of-claims-free years, respectively.

Regulating Health Care Professionals Educational Costs

The U.S. Department of Education would calculate costs for providing courses, laboratories, etc.; i.e., the costs associated with each segment/course of study for the health care professions, and utilize a similar methodology as insurers use to cap services, to cap educational costs for health professionals.

The U.S. Department of Education would also take over all existing outstanding health professionals' loans from private corporations, and would be the sole provider of all future loans, eliminating private sector involvement.

Interest rates accruing while the student is still enrolled full or part time would be set at a fixed 1%. Interest rates would be brought to a fixed 3% 1 year after graduation and remain at 3% throughout the payback period.

The principle amount of all loan payments by health care professionals would be fully tax deductible for the entire payback period; the interest portion of these payments would not be deductible.

∞

If you choose to believe that mandated health insurance is never to happen, look carefully at your auto insurance. In many states, personal injury coverage for you and others is mandated. This is mandated health insurance!

We are also seeing our federal government begin medical malpractice litigation capitation/reform.

I would suggest that, at this time, the wheels are well into motion for the formation of something very similar to what you have just read.

As this book goes to print, Massachusetts is about to become the first state to REQUIRE all citizens to purchase health insurance in one way or another…the above is becoming a reality!

Whether or not you choose to take care of yourself and lead a healthy lifestyle is your decision and your right, as well.

But, health insurance and health care has devolved into a selective institution with only the well-off and the corporate employee able to afford it and access it.

With multitudes of Americans moving into the self-employed/sole-proprietor status, and with the previously stated statistics in mind, it is more than apparent that such a system, or something similar, will truly have to be formulated in order to bring about the dramatic changes of better health and of making health insurance and health care *affordable* and *accessible* to *all* Americans; not just the corporate employee, the well-off, children, and our elders.

I do truly believe that the vast majority in civilized, developed Western countries have lost, or perhaps have never had to begin with, the two most important ingredients to attaining and maintaining a life of optimum health on all levels regardless of their economic level. Those two ingredients are *Self* and *Respect.*

Dr. David Robinson

PART II

HOW to Make A Total Transformation of Your Life

&

Make It Last For the Rest of Your Life

3

Nutrition For Health

Start with daily nutrition and gut the gluttony.

Look at your daily food intake. Now, look at the *Food Pyramid.* How does your nutrition stack up? Does the Pyramid reverse? You need to evolve your eating habits closer and closer to the *Food Pyramid* until it is part of your daily nutrition. Then, raise the bar on it a little!

Gradually end all diets & diet supplements and begin using the *Food Pyramid* for daily nutrition, meals, and snacks. This is scientifically researched with major benefits to health and longevity.

Start with one day per week and, every 2 weeks, add on another day until you reach 7 days a week.

To keep hunger at bay, change to eating 4 – 6 smaller meals each day, beginning about 30 minutes after rising, continuing every 3 hours thereafter. Make your last meal approximately ninety minutes before retiring, and make it your smallest with the least carbohydrates, leaning more toward proteins.

This pattern allows for the best digestion, maximum utilization of foods and their nutrients by the body, and the most efficient elimination of wastes.

Choose nutritional supplements which contain the following combination of ingredients. For most, it is far more important that you just get the Multi-Vitamin Multi-Mineral Supplement with as close to the Daily Value as possible. Note: *More is not better!* The D.V. is established for a reason: for every day use by the average adult. Other elements should be utilized in the combinations set forth below, or containing as many elements as possible. Do not purchase single elements as they tend to have higher concentrations in the supplement. Although a D.V. may not be established for particular elements, the combination supplements will contain amounts that are sufficient for use by the body.

Always check with your pharmacist and physician for possible interactions with any medications your taking or any conditions you have *prior* to beginning use of any of these supplements.

The brand you choose should be a premium brand, not a store brand.

I. Multi-Vitamin/Multi-Mineral Supplement

- Vitamin A {Beta Carotene}
- Vitamin C
- Vitamin D {Fish Liver Oil}
- Vitamin E {d-Alph/Beta/Gamma/Delta Tocopherols}
- Vitamin B1 {Thiamine}
- Vitamin B2 {Riboflavin}
- Vitamin B3 {Niacin}
- Vitamin B6 {Pyridoxine}
- Vitamin B12 {Cyanocobalamin}
- Folic Acid
- Biotin
- Pantothenic Acid
- Calcium {Calcium Carbonate/Dicalcium Phosphate}
- Iron {Ferrous Fumarate}
- Phosphorus
- Iodine

- Magnesium
- Zinc
- Selenium
- Copper
- Manganese
- Chromium
- Potassium
- Boron

II. Whole Food – Flora Supplement

- Rutin
- Citrus Bioflavanoid
- PABA
- Royal Jelly
- Bee Pollen
- Bee Propolis
- Choline Bipartrate
- Inositol
- Octacosanol
- Soy Lecithin
- DNA
- RNA
- Coenzyme Q
- EPA {Eicosapentaenois Acid}
- DHA {Docosahexaenoic Acid}
- Chlorophyll

III. Antioxidant Supplement

- Pychnogenol

- Quercitin
- Green Tea Extract
- Echinacea
- Bilberry
- Schizandra
- Barley Powder
- Broccoli Powder
- Spirulina
- Chlorella
- Citrus Fiber

A daily complete Amino Acid supplement at your last meal is highly recommended.

Amino Acids are the building blocks for most regenerative, growth, and maintenance processes of the body.

They are essential for muscle/tendon/ligament functions & maintenance.

IV. Amino Acids

- L-Alanine
- L-Arginine
- L-Aspartic Acid
- L-Leucine
- L-Lysine
- L-Methionine
- L-Carnitine
- L-Phenylalanine
- L-Proline
- L-Serine
- L-Threonine

- L-Tryptophan
- L-Tyrosine
- L-Valine
- L-Ornithine
- L-Glutamic Acid
- L-Glycine
- L-Histadine
- L-Isoleucine

In order to maximize bio-availability {the amount your body absorbs} and bio-utilization {the amount your body uses from what it has absorbed}, here are some recommendations.

II & III are taken with your morning meal. I & IV are taken with your evening meal.

Never take any supplements on an empty stomach; the bio-availability and bio-utilization will be negligible.

An acidophilus supplement with your 1st meal is essential as well, for maintaining the good bacteria of the digestive system that is involved in digesting foods properly.

That 12oz glass of H_2O at each meal is not to be forgotten. Water is the essential ingredient for all bodily functions.

As far as food goes, it would be better if you could purchase whole foods and organic food.

Their nutrient content is believed to be higher, besides being guaranteed a dramatic decrease in the ingestion of harmful chemicals.

Another addition to your diet is soy products; a healthy food source rich in isoflavanoids.

Let's tackle the 'tastes good, bad for you' stuff.

Alcohol. Max it out at one 12-ounce glass per day. Here, you gain the benefits of decreasing the risk of heart diseases and save yourself from potential liver and kidney problems later in life.

Severely limit and restrict your intake of packaged snack foods, junk foods, and processed foods. Eliminating them altogether is best, but, if you must indulge, a max of one to two servings per week is recommended.

This decreases your ingestion of harmful fats, additives, artificial ingredients and preservatives, which decreases your risk of heart and artery diseases and various forms of intestinal conditions and cancers.

You'll also have better-looking skin, your largest organ, which must be fed like all other organs. Only, it's on the outside.

Soft drinks are no more than glorified potential diabetes in a can! Eliminate them…Period! You'll greatly decrease the risk of diabetes and obesity as well as decrease the ingestion of artificial ingredients.

A word on all these fad diets. FORGET THEM! Your body WAS designed to utilize ALL basic food groups PROPERLY as fuel when you have BALANCED INTAKE of each of them and do not overindulge in any one group.

Simply follow the new *Food Pyramid* and its accompanying directions, as published by the Harvard School of Public Health (this is available on-line), and then tweak it as per above.

Shattering the myth of "quick-fix" diets and proving how they DO NOT work is easy.

Severely restricting caloric intake triggers your body to perceive starvation. This causes the body to adapt to the restricted calories by “lightening the load” via shedding its most “weighty” tissue; muscle.

Muscle is the most metabolically active tissue of the body, so the less muscle you have, the less food you need.

Thus, reducing muscle tissue also reduces the metabolic activity of the body.

Since fat is only burned by metabolic activity, the body now stores fat more readily because of this reduced metabolism.

You may achieve your desired weight, but you have done so primarily as a result of lost muscle tissue, as well as fat.

When the diet ends, because of the loss of the metabolically active tissue (muscle) and, thus, the decreased ability to burn fat, fat becomes far more readily stored. In other words, the fat “comes right back” and, usually, fast!

So, forget all the fads, potions, and fixes. Eat real. Eat right. And eat to live, don’t live to eat!

Now a hardball word on tobacco and illicit/illegal drugs. It is nothing more than injecting illness into your body, quick and easy. If you’re not into major disease and suffering or death, somehow, some way, GET OFF IT!! Not using has many benefits. Some of the subtler ones are dramatically decreasing your risk of many types of cancers, heart/lung diseases, circulation and vascular problems, and psychological/emotional problems.

This is your new nutrition. This is what you fuel your body with, so make it grade A, high octane. You will thank yourself for it in the long run. Would you put kerosene in your car? Would you expect it to run properly or for long on kerosene? Then treat your body with the SAME respect when it comes to fueling IT!

NOTES

4

Exorcise the Sloth to Waste the Waist

The formula for this is quite simple. Real Fitness = strength training + aerobic training. The plan to implement the formula entails education, commitment, effort, conviction, and fortitude. The plan works like this:

Education first.

It is no wonder that the following information has received 18 rejection letters from numerous *popular culture* health and fitness magazines.

The desperate journalists of these pop-culture magazines have continually touted one *quick-fix, lose fat fast* approach after another as they fight for readers and clamor to feed the public's insatiable thirst for overnight changes in their bodies.

The pictures of all those 'body beautiful' models that supplement those articles place the idea that such approaches are great and work wonderfully.

All of this done in the face of mountains of medical research dictating, for years, that quick fix approaches are potentially harmful and unhealthy *and* mostly worthless.

Now, finally, the FDA and FTC have just publicly denounced the use of such *magic drugs, rubs, lotions and potions* to *get 'fit' quick* and *lose fat fast,* as unhealthy, unsafe, *and*, mostly nonsense. They are now committed to bringing an end to these hucksters' false claims.

But what has been seen immediately following this statement

by the FDA and FTC? Barrages of ¼ to ½ page advertisements touting get *fit quick, lose fat fast*! Why? Because these marketers know that Americans have the addiction to get 'fit' quickly and lose fat fast. These marketers have wrongly convinced the public that 'fit' means 'weight loss' and 'being thin'. They know most Americans' compulsive nature when it comes to losing weight. They want the *magic bullets*, the *fast fitness* via *magic drugs, rubs, lotions and potions* to get them looking good fast.

The public has been blinded by the sophistry of *thin and svelte equals healthy and fit,* and, that they can achieve this *in just 10 days!* So, they continue to buy into one foolish scheme after another, time after time, to achieve this end, regardless of any consequences to their health.

Usually, the *magic fast track fat formula* fails, and the person then bails out from its use, frustrated again, duped again. It is no wonder that the *fail-'n-bail* cycle is ever-so-prevalent in our society in the fight against fat.

The core problem is this misinformation the public has been fed.

Getting fit is not just being *svelte*. *Getting* fit is really just the tip of the iceberg.

Commitment, Conviction, Effort, and Fortitude are next.

Beyond *getting* fit is the *real* challenge: *staying fit for life, making fitness a lifestyle.* Staying fit for life requires *commitment* for life...to a changed schedule, changed nutritional habits, changed attitudes, changed priorities.

This entails requirements and responsibilities; words that are the antithesis of *quick fix* and *magic*, when it comes to *real* fitness.

Spending a minimum of three times a week for an hour to 90 minutes sweating and working out, along with eating-habit changes, to achieve looking good and being svelte is a process much too slow and arduous for the frenzied public. But, it is the correct way. It is the only way for *lasting*, *healthy* changes in body contour.

To begin with, let's change the mindset from a *fight against* fat to a *commitment for* fitness and health. Fighting is exhausting and weakening. Commitment *for* a positive change is empowering and energizing.

Now, let's plow-under the fat farmers, stow their wears in the barn permanently, and get down to the basic truth about losing fat.

Step one: Affirm Your Commitment.

Acquire a *knowing* (*belief* leaves room for doubt!) that you are going to do, and will continue to do, whatever it takes to make fitness a part of your lifestyle *for life!* However you go about this is your choice.

Step two: Educate Yourself.

Weight loss and body beautiful is more often than not the number one desired goal. When someone says this is their goal, they typically diet.

Since that rapid decline of the numbers on the scale is due to your losing both fat *and* muscle, you've got a real serious problem, because you've just lost part of the machinery (muscle) you need to *burn fat and calories from the foods you eat!* It's the muscle that puts the proper contours to your body, whereas fat is usually unsightly.

Simply put, you have to maintain or increase lean body

tissue (muscle) while decreasing body fat. That means changing and cleaning up those nutritional habits.

Physiologically, strength training uses a carbohydrate stored in your body (glycogen) for its energy source. Aerobic training first uses glycogen, then, when this source is depleted, body fat is burned. So, ideally, when you begin your fitness/exercise routine, after having eaten properly and stored that glycogen, you'll have the ability to have a great strength workout, use up the glycogen, and, with your heart rate already elevated, begin your aerobic workout and almost immediately be in the fat-burning stage!

Step three: Change.

Take your daily schedule and lay it out in weekly format in front of you. There *are*, at the *very* least, four hours where certain things can be delegated to someone else, reduced in frequency or duration, or eliminated altogether. No excuses! Much of our time is wasted on frivolous activity. So, get tough: purge the fluff!

Step four: Join a Fitness Club.

Correct, *join a fitness center.* This is one of the biggest hurdles for many people, but, in my professional opinion, – and many of my colleagues are not as emphatic about this – it is one of the *biggest* necessities. This is another part of your commitment; the financial/psychological commitment.

Affordability is always a concern. But how many lunches and dinners out all month do you 'afford'? How much weekly entertainment do you 'afford'? I don't buy this excuse unless you're in some really hard financial straights. Besides, this *is not* an expense. It is a *direct investment* in your health.

You need to keep *motivated* as well. Going it alone for the exercise neophyte usually leads to boredom, doubt, excuses; and this leads to bail-'n-fail.

Meeting other people like yourself and being in an environment totally geared to fitness keeps you connected, and this will keep you encouraged and positive.

And, as far as those excuses about embarrassment and being intimidated are concerned…dump them! If you spend your life worrying about what everyone else thinks of you, you're like a prisoner! Prisoners can't do things because they're locked behind walls. Fear sets up mental walls, preventing you from doing things. What's the difference? So, get over it and get into it (a fitness center).

Also, make sure the center you choose has certified fitness staff (personal trainers, aerobics instructors).

Step five: *Just Do It* Right Now*!*

You've accomplished steps 1 – 4; you're in the fitness center, joining up. Step 3 enters the picture. Purge the fluff and *Let's roll!* You should have your workout clothes on and be ready to work out the moment after the staff member says, "Welcome aboard."

Remember, the last thing any center wants is an injured or frustrated new member. They quit. So, don't be shy. Then and there, inquire about complimentary training sessions. Being new to fitness, they know that you *need* guidance and direction from one of their trainers on what to do and how to do it. You *will* get it then and there.

These are five, no magic, requiring commitment and sacrifice steps that will lead to *real* fitness, *real* health, great looks and longevity; priceless benefits for your body, your mind, your state-of-health.

You are now on your way toward a whole new life, a whole new you. No magic. No nonsense. Just commitment, effort, conviction, fortitude, and "miracles."

Strength training should be done 3 times every week with a day of rest between each workout day. A full body workout each time is best for the beginner.

Warm up with 10 repetitions of light weights for each muscle, using weights that you can easily finish the reps with, with minimal muscle fatigue. This is a light, full-body workout.

Next, perform 1 set of 10 – 12 repetitions for each muscle, using weight that you can just finish the last repetition with, with light muscle fatigue. Nothing here is heavy weight. Neophytes get injured that way.

Keep it simple. Keep it smart.

Continue on with this routine, adding 5 lbs to the weight used every 3 – 4 weeks.

Stop adding weight when you reach a point of finishing the 2nd set of 10 reps with moderate muscle fatigue.

Now the fun begins.

The idea is, without going into a dissertation on exercise physiology, to keep your body guessing.

Muscles get used to the same routine and the benefits of a strength workout fade. So, change up and alternate the weight used and the *order* of the muscles you train every 2 – 3 weeks. Also, learn new strength training exercises and use your body weight (push-ups, pull-ups, dips), too.

The aerobic training part must not be forgotten.

This is the buddy system, and, without aerobics, strength training is just half a person! If you can handle it, follow your strength training with 60 minutes of aerobic training 3 times each week. Otherwise, alternate your strength and aerobic training days.

The code for aerobic training must not be broken, or *you* risk getting broken.

Start with a 10-minute warm up of slow paced walking. That's *your* normal stride. Then, it's off to the races with 5 to 10 minutes of gradually increased intensity, working up to 40 minutes at your maximum heart rate.

Fitness centers and their staff can inform you about heart rates. The idea here is to get you into it. The cool down follows with 10 minutes of gradually decreasing intensity.

Aerobic training comes in all forms and shapes and colors. There are aerobics classes, cardio machines, in-line skating, running, power-walking, swimming, biking, tennis, martial arts, hiking, kayaking. Just choose your weapon.

A martial rule within the aerobic code: drink a minimum of 16 oz of water 1 hour prior to exercise and hydrate sensibly (*sip* water) throughout exercise!

Your last food & supplements should be ingested a minimum of 90 minutes prior to exercise.

Like strength training, aerobic training should be changed up and alternated every 3 – 4 weeks.

Now, just watch that body respond!

NOTES

5

Real Rest for Power & Productivity

If you're eating properly and exercising regularly, not getting proper amounts of sleep is going to minimize all the benefits.

Sleep is when the body regenerates, rejuvenates, and recharges. That's right: you're a biological battery.

The minimum amount of time needed by most people is 6 hours of sleep each night. This allows your body to repair all the "harm" done to its physiological processes and its nervous system during the waking hours.

Benefits of proper sleep include increased mental alertness and awareness, decreased daytime fatigue, enhanced immune function, increased physical capabilities and stamina, help to maintain the natural rhythm of the body's physiology at proper speed and in proper balance, help to maintain the body's biological clock, and help to prevent illness and maintain your mood in the "good" mode; helping you to deal with the day's little curve balls better. Ever dealt with a cranky coworker, family member, friend who does not get enough sleep? Enough said!

But, also realize that a maximum amount of sleep exists.

For the majority of people, nine hours of sleep each night should not be surpassed. Any more than this and the results can be physical and mental sluggishness all day long. Your body's processes never "recover" from the excess sleep; think of it as having taken a tranquilizer. The body's processes never "gear up" for the day. Understand that there are exceptions to this, depending upon someone's degree/level of activities of daily living (stress, physical/mental). But, generally, this is a good rule of thumb to follow.

As well, ensuring proper bedding (mattress and pillow) for your sleep enhances the quality of your sleep (continuous, uninterrupted) and helps to prevent back problems and joint soreness.

NOTES

“What a man’s mind can conceive of and believe in, it can achieve”

Napoleon Hill

6

Mindfulness & Inspiration

Let us not forget that essential body part above the shoulders. As much as the mind and brain is exercised, it, too, needs rest.

Meditation, quiet time, down time, call it whatever you like, it is essential. It allows the brain waves, which may be likened to a stormy, frothing sea when you are awake, to reach a calm state when you meditate. Meditation is not like sleep. Meditation is going down inside the mind and body semi-consciously; unlike sleep, which is unconscious.

Numerous books and tapes exist on the subject. Check them out for an in-depth explanation if you so desire.

It is recommended that you meditate an average of 3 to 4 times each week for 30 – 60 minutes. Here are some easy to use methods:

Be seated comfortably and still, alone and in a quite place where you will not be disturbed.

Be in or imagine your favorite place (room, woods, beach, mountains, desert, fields).

Have your eyes closed and project a black background.

Focus on your heartbeat *only* for 5 minutes; no thoughts.

Breathe in slowly, count to 3, and see the word RELAX. Then, breathe out slowly and see the word DEEP.

Do this for 5 sets.

Now, imagine yourself entering an elevator. The doors close. See the number 5 against your black background in front of you as you stand in the elevator.

Feel yourself begin to descend and see the numbers move downward in front of you from 5 to 1.

At level 1, see the elevator doors open, walk out into your favorite place; your sanctuary.

Stay relaxed, calm, peaceful.

Feel yourself begin to float off the ground. Imagine yourself floating around your sanctuary, peaceful, happy, healthy. Notice every little detail of your sanctuary. Take it all in.

Float back down to the ground and return to elevator.

See the doors open, enter the elevator. See the doors close, slowly ascend from level 1 to level 5.

See the doors open. Exit the elevator.

Slowly, begin to feel yourself at your present place.

Take 3 slow, deep breaths. Now, open your eyes.

Enjoy the ride?

Here is an alternate technique for those less tranquil:

Go to your favorite outdoor nature-place, alone, undisturbed, seated or lying comfortably.

Focus and concentrate only on your surroundings; the sights, the sounds, the smells, the feelings on your face and body; no other thoughts.

Remain there in that state-of-mind for 30 to 60 minutes.

The intricacies and details that surround us that we overlook everyday are amazing!

If you need a little help getting started, here's another way to meditate:

Sitting or lying in a favorite place, chair, couch, use a headset and listen to a tape or CD of tranquil 'meditating' music or sounds of nature.

Keep your eyes closed and focus only on the tape music or sounds. Concentrate on how they make you feel inside.

Take five deep breaths, following the same steps outlined in the first example, going through the imagery as previously described.

Have a nice trip!

Meditation is not the only thing you can do to set that mindset to a positive mode and de-stress.

Affirmations work in subtle ways to help achieve this end. 'Prayer' is what you may wish to call it. I use the two interchangeably.

Begin the daily practice of saying one positive affirmation about yourself, your life, or any aspect about daily living, nature or God (or however you wish to focus). Make them up or use some that you've read in a spiritual text or book. Write them on 3 inch by 5 inch index cards and pick one per day or week to repeat throughout the day, particularly upon arising in the morning. The benefits are quite simple but very healthy for body, mind, and spirit.

Saying and keeping positive affirmations in mind throughout the day helps to reduce blood pressure and anxiety, increase secretion of 'good mood' brain chemicals, increase peace of mind, slow down and focus the thought process, reduce fatigue, increase positive mental attitude, increase clear thinking, increase self confidence and self image.

There is so much negative print to read in this world, so shift gears and begin to delve into spiritually-based books & authors, like Wayne Dyer, Deepak Chopra, John Randolph Price, Stuart Wilde, and others. You may also choose the spiritual text of your choice. You can incorporate this into your meditation if desired.

The main point is to establish a regular practice of reading such positive books a minimum of 10 minutes daily, just like reading the newspaper. This helps to increase and regenerate a sense of hope, peace-of-mind, and faith in self & others.

Quite frankly, you may find it increases your awareness, appreciation, and acceptance of all life and of all people.

NOTES

7

Downshifting

Daily life has evolved to dizzying speeds and unrealistic levels of seriousness. This, too, is unhealthy. So, enjoy your life a little more than you have been.

Creativity is an essential ingredient that must be mixed into life, or life can become a bit stale and a bit too real. Creativity is another need in you that must be satisfied.

Engage in a hobby, outdoor activity, or recreational/creative interest (outside of television, stereo, video) of your choice and liking for a minimum of 3 times each week for about 60 minutes. (Sort of sounds like a sex therapist recommendation!).

Some very simple benefits include entertainment, fun, and enjoyment, as well as providing a healthy change that improves your attitude and disposition. Regular R-'n-R makes the routine activities of daily living seem less mundane and more tolerable.

Downshifting your life a bit can lead you to a more peaceful place, too. Begin to delegate and prioritize items on your "to do" list to others. This gives others a little more responsibility and gives you a little less stress.

When you're leaving to go *anywhere,* leave in time to be able to take your time to arrive on time. This means no speeding, no rushing, and more of <u>*less*</u> stress. Be aware of your distances and travel times.

Try to plan and schedule in a straight (one-way) line when doing chores or errands, etc.; in other words don't go "back

& forth."

Start a daily practice of rising ½ hour to 1 hour earlier each morning, giving you more time to "do things" at a less hectic pace.

You can also learn a few pace-slowing "secrets," like begin to say "no, thank you" when time is tight and/or ask for help in doing things.

The bottom line is to try your level best to plan and schedule efficiently enough so that you can "take it easy" while "getting things done," and not overloading yourself with "doing it all now."

Rushing around being "busy" may be the current day "prestigious" thing to do, but its toll on your ticker and mindset is extremely negative. And all for what? To be "in," "stylish?" Bunk! Be sensible.

NOTES

8

Health and Lifestyle Evaluation

Now for the really hard part.

This is the reality check where people become acutely aware of just how less-than-at-good-to-excellent health they are. This is a general formula I devised as a way of grading your overall health. Just like school, it's time to get tested. This is time-consuming. But, if you're reading this book, then you possess a level of value about your health that less than 35% of the population of this country has. So, sit down and dig in.

Step I: Current Health Review

Complete the following and record on paper the results and/or information:

1. Complete physical examination & review of systems

2. Blood & urine lab workups

3. Electrocardiogram

4. Stress test

5. Fitness assessment

6. Chiropractic evaluation (spine)

7. Mental/emotional health evaluation

8. Occupation hazards exposure (chemical, physical, emotional, risk of types of injury) review

9. Health history review (previous illnesses, conditions, diseases)

10. Family health history review (previous and present illnesses, conditions, diseases for immediate family [parents, grandparents, great grandparents, siblings])

11. Activities of daily living risk taking (speeding, aggressive driving, not utilizing a seatbelt, use of cell phone while driving, j-walking, walking against 'don't walk' signs).

12. R-'n-R and hobby risks taking (sky diving, hang gliding, rock climbing, any type of auto/boat racing, scuba diving, bungee jumping, extreme sports)

Step II: Present Lifestyle Review:

1. Nutrition

a. Poor = follow the recommendations in chapter 3 *never to rarely.*

b. Fair = follow the chapter 3 recommendations *sometimes.*

c. Good = follow the chapter 3 recommendations *frequently.*

d. Excellent = follow the chapter 3 recommendations *often.*

e. Superior = follow the chapter 3 recommendations *always.*

2. Fitness

a. Poor = follow the recommendations in chapters 4 and 5 1 time per week or less.

b. Fair = follow the chapters 4 and 5 recommendations 2 times per week.

c. Good = follow the chapters 4 and 5 recommendations 3 times per week.

d. Excellent = follow the chapters 4 and 5 recommendations 4 times per week.

e. Superior = follow the chapters 4 and 5 recommendations 5+ times per week.

3. Mind and Spirit

a. Poor = follow chapters 6 and 7 recommendations 1 time per week or less.

b. Fair = follow the chapters 6 and 7 recommendations 2 – 3 times per week.

c. Good = follow the chapters 6 and 7 recommendations 4 – 5 times per week.

d. Excellent = follow the chapters 6 and 7 recommendations 6 –7 times per week.

e. Superior = follow the chapters 6 and 7 recommendations 7+ times per week.

4. Sleep

a. Poor = an average of less than 4 hours or more than 8 hours of sleep per night.

b. Fair = an average of 4 hours of sleep per night.

c. Good = an average of 5 hours of sleep per night.

d. Excellent = an average of 6 hours of sleep per night.

e. Superior = an average of 7 – 8 hours of sleep per night.

5. Recreation-Hobby

a. Poor = an average of 60 minutes less than 1 x week.

b. Fair = an average of 60 minutes 1 x week.

c. Good = an average of 60 minutes 2 x week.

d. Excellent = an average of 60 minutes 3 x week.

e. Superior = an average of 60 minutes 4+ x week.

Step III: Overall Health & Lifestyle Evaluation:

Superior Health = Step I has 0 positives/affirmatives and Step II #1 – 5 has 4+ *Superior* and the remainder are *Excellent.*

Excellent Health = Step I has 1 positive/affirmative and Step II #1 – 5 has 3 *Excellent* and the remainder are *Good* to *Superior.*

Good Health = Step I has 2 – 3 positives/affirmatives and Step II #1 – 5 has 3 *Good* and the remainder are *Fair* to *Superior.*

Fair Health = Step I has 3-4 positives/affirmatives and Step II #1 – 5 has 3 *Fair* and the remainder are *Poor to Excellent.*

Poor Health = Step I has 4 – 5 positives/affirmations and Step II #1 – 5 has 3 *Poor* and the remainder are *Fair* to *Good.*

Un-Healthy = Step I has +5 positives/affirmatives and Step II # 1 – 5 has 4+ *Poor* and the remainder are *Fair.*

Where do you "size" up? Over 60% of the U.S. population falls within the range of *Un-Healthy* to *Fair* health. Deplorable. With all the resources available in this country that percentage should be <u>no</u> higher than 20%. End of discussion.

NOTES

9

Ensuring Personalized Coverage

Health insurance is no bargain and not very easy to understand, regardless of the company, group, or policy. The basic American attitude of "more is better" prevails, and it costs individuals and families thousands of dollars each year in unnecessary health expenses, both in care and in coverage.

Here is a way to get *real* health care and the health coverage you *need*:

First, you must evaluate your results from chapter 8 to determine your level of health and lifestyle.

If you are in *excellent* to *superior* health, then you have little use of the health care system because you are rarely ill or injured.

This indicates that you *need* only a *Major Sickness & Accident* or *Catastrophic Care* coverage.

Even if you are in the *excellent* to *superior* category, and even if you are well informed and familiar with natural and herbal remedies, consider pharmaceutical coverage. The final judgment is yours.

A *Comprehensive* policy is surely a waste of money for you. The "what ifs" are covered under *Major Sickness & Accident* policies. A safeguard is to increase your auto insurance *medical expenses* to at least $50,000 per accident.

It is also wise to establish a *Personal Health Care Savings Account* for other health care expenses that you will pay for out of pocket (O.O.P.). How much money to place in such an account is discussed later.

You should not be shy about asking providers, who you must pay for O.O.P., about *cash-paid-at-time-of-service reduced fees*. Many providers are very cooperative on this front.

If you are in *good* health, then you do utilize the health care system occasionally. So, your needs for insurance coverage are a little more generous; like HMO, PPO, and Point Of Service plans.

A *Comprehensive* policy is still unnecessary and a waste of money for you. You may consider the purchase of a separate *Hospital Indemnity* plan from a separate carrier that pays a level amount per day directly to you while hospitalized.

Being below *superior/excellent* health, consider keeping pharmaceutical coverage. Catastrophic events often require the use of life-saving and expensive drugs. Again, increase your auto insurance *Medical Expenses* to a minimum of $50,000 per accident. And, do establish a *Personal Health Care Savings Account* for those O.O.P. health care expenses.

If you are in *fair* to *unhealthy* health, then your needs for health care may be great to excessive.

If you are ineligible for Medicare and/or Medicaid/State Health, then you *need* a *Comprehensive* policy and a *Hospital Indemnity* policy from a separate carrier. You should also seriously consider a *Long Term Care* policy that has a *home health care provision* (a consideration for all levels of health).

Once you have determined where your needs lie as far as health insurance is concerned, next is some number crunching for establishing a *Personal Health Care Savings Account.* The following seven steps give you an estimated yearly amount to keep in your *PHCSA.*

1. Add up all health care expenses paid O.O.P. each year for last five years. Average the five years O.O.P. expenses. This amount is #1.

2. List all health care services not covered under your chosen policy.

   a. Contact all providers of choice for the fees they charge for the services you will utilize.

   b. Estimate your # of visits for a one year period that will be paid O.O.P. to each provider that is not covered under your policy.

3. Add up these (#1 + #2) O.O.P. fee expenses.

4. Estimate your # of visits to providers that are covered under your chosen policy

5. Add up all the Co-payments and Deductibles for these providers for the year.

6. Add the totals from #3, and #5 together.

7. Calculate 5% of this total and add this % to your original total (#3 + #5).

The amount you now have (#7) is the yearly minimum amount that you need to hold in your *PHCSA.* The question always comes up; *Where is this money going to come from?*

From you and your <u>*changed*</u> lifestyle and habit-patterns, and from the realization that *health* can need care *immediately*, whereas retirement is a futuristic endeavor and entertainment secondary. In other words, you need monetary coverage for your O.O.P. health expenses NOW, in the event that these expenses become reality NOW. Here are some ideas for sources for your *PHCSA:*

- Reduce by 25% the amount of money regularly put into retirement account(s) and put this amount into your *PHCSA.* Do this until the needed minimum is established in your *PHCSA.*
- Liquidate stocks, bonds, luxury items (yes, cars, boats, jewelry, etc.), and household items.
- Reduce entertainment by at least 50%, placing the money saved into your *PHCSA* on a regular basis just as you would spend the money on entertainment.
- Take a 2nd job if you're able to, temporarily, and save all money for deposit into your *PHCSA.*

A word of advice: consult a Certified Public Accountant for the best no-risk savings vehicles with which to start your *PHCSA*. D*o not* consult a financial planner or investment adviser or stockbroker or insurance broker about a *PHCSA*, no matter how much they claim to know. Their interest is in *their* profit, not your ability and need to pay for health expenses.

NOTES

10

SELF INSURING with REAL HEALTH CARE

This is what I term *Lifestyle as Health Insurance*, and is how I have conducted my adult life. This is only recommended for those who religiously follow an *Excellent* to *Superior* lifestyle, as previously evaluated.

First, you must select providers for *preventive* and *maintenance* care of your *Excellent* to *Superior* health. Here, I suggest the following providers on a rotating monthly basis:

- Chiropractor (D.C.)
- Acupuncturist (Li. Ac.)
- Massage Therapist (L.M.T.)

You may also choose to utilize a Certified Reiki Therapist and/or Reflexologist. (This being the year 2006, conjecture, prejudice and disdain have no place! Get educated, *get over it*, and get on with using these health-enhancing assets!)

Second, it also imperative that you receive periodic (yearly) health checks from the various medical providers you have chosen. As well, preventive dental care and eye exams are received every six months.

Third, utilize only natural, nutritional, herbal and botanical remedies for illness, symptoms, or conditions immediately upon their onset. Pharmaceuticals are utilized only when rare, extreme, or persistently worsening conditions or illnesses occur.

Fourth, your only need for health care insurance will arise from a catastrophic event. Thus, the only health insurance purchased is a *Catastrophic Care* policy.

Your automobile insurance *Medical Payments* must be increase to its maximum, and as well, purchase any optional *Medical Payments* coverage available up to the available maximum.

Lastly, transfer the necessary amounts of stocks, bonds, investments, and savings into a *PHCSA* to reach your needed minimum.

This may all seem very drastic to you unless you are at and maintain that *Excellent* to *Superior* level of health and lifestyle. Then, it all makes sense because *good health* is your primary value, primary asset, and primary responsibility. This *is* a value system transformation away from what most of society has become “stuck-in-their-stuff” with and find it impossible to let go of.

NOTES

NOTES

PART III

FROM "IMPOSSIBLE"

To

*I'M*POSSIBLE

11

Walking the Talk

I probably represent about 3% of the American population today, based on the lifestyle I have lead since 22 years of age. That may be 3% of the population based on lifestyle, but, if you add in my value system and the way I know and believe what most humans are capable of, I bet I go off the radar screen, so to speak!

Exercise?

Today, I generally warm up with a fast paced walk for 1 mile, do a full body stretching routine, then I will go through one full body training circuit of 1 set of 7 – 10 reps for each muscle group using light weight or my body weight, then do 3 core-training exercises of 1 set of 12 reps using only body weight, then another full body training circuit with different exercises/machines, and then do cardio with 30 minutes on the "random" setting, level 9 – 10 of the stationary bike or treadmill, ending with a full body stretch routine; different stretches. That's done 2 days each week on alternate days and 3 other days, I'll hit a Tae-Bo, STEP, or Yoga class.

Nutrition?

Rather simple, really. I stay away from all the "whites"; flour, sugar, milk, with alcohol in extreme moderation, and take to the new *Food Pyramid*, eating organic or natural whenever possible and adding soy milk and tofu several times each week. But, one day a week, I'll eat-as-I-please to some extent…pizza, lasagna, ice cream, but in moderation. I don't gorge till I'm stuffed.

Plenty of water is essential with each meal – 12 ounces – and throughout the day, as well as pre and post exercise.

Supplements?

They are a daily *multi-vitamin/multi-mineral/whole foods* tablet with my evening meal. As well, 90 minutes pre workout, I take CoEnzyme Q and an a botanical anti-oxidant capsule. 30 minutes post training, I'll take a complete amino acid supplement. I never take mega-doses and generally go for the low to moderate side of amounts. As well, I don't do meds; I use herbal supplements when basic illness strikes…it's always worked, but I have become well-versed in their use and would not recommend use of them by anyone unless they study up first…it's not easy material.

Rest ? Relaxation? Recreation?

Meditation at least 30 minutes daily, sleep 7 hours a night. On days off: a 60 minute walk on the beach or in the woods, reading from the spiritual masters past and present, watching a fire (in the woodstove or fireplace of course!), gardening, landscaping, roller-blading, kayaking, furniture refinishing …sounds like it's still exercise, doesn't it?

Spirituality?

No religion. To me, it has been and remains a direct cause of many woes in many nations around the globe…it's just a "knowing" I have that there is a "Source" or "Universal Intelligence" which has a direct extension into all living things as an "Innate Intelligence," and this is what I focus on in daily meditation. (This whole nonsense of Intelligent Design vs. Evolution…Evolution *is* Intelligent Design… name anything in nature that occurs spontaneously… lightning, natural disasters, it all has an underlying, hidden cause that *takes time* before there is a manifestation that we can sense!*...don't they get it?*!)

Real Health Care?

Chiropractic spinal adjustments every 3 weeks, alternating massage and acupuncture every other month, dental cleaning per 6 months, yearly medical physical exam, eye exam yearly and I will go to a local dermatologist's yearly offer to the public of a free skin cancer screening.

Health Insurance?

I have a moderate savings account set up as I indicated in Chapter 8, which I use as my minor and usual health care expenses dictate (PHCSA).

A catastrophic health insurance plan is in place and I am constantly on the lookout for better, less costly ones.

What good is all this going to do anyway? I'll bet that if I submitted myself to some rigorous testing – blood, urine, hair, stress test, ECG, etc. to any university Health Science & Fitness center, my biological age would be a good ten years less than my chronological age, which basically means I can do just about anything someone who is 35 can do at peak performance....Now that's *living* life!

∞

So, just who do I think I am to make such statements and write a book endorsing *Mandatory Minimum Merit-Rated Health Insurance,* and about how to make dramatic changes and be healthy in all aspects of your life and lifestyle?

I am more than happy to divulge that to you. Perhaps, by knowing my very humble beginnings, you will come to realize why I have such nonconformist, but extremely passionate views that buck today's apathetic status quo.

In the beginning, *I* was a grossly obese child with all the accoutrements of being always sick-'n-tired...purely unhealthy!

By the age of 12, I began to drive myself to better myself physically by undertaking swimming and gymnastics at the local YMCA.

By age 22, I had the opportunity to be involved in health and health care. I was able to see and to know just how unhealthy the vast majority of people really are. It changed me – in all ways – dramatically.

I chose to pursue a lifestyle of good health on all levels; body mind and spirit, from fitness to daily living.

Today, I retain the same lifestyle because I love life, I love its experiences, and I desire to live them to the fullest every day of my life.

Being in a state of *less than healthy* would not allow me to do this.

But, I have paid a price for this lifestyle. Socially, if I've heard it once, I've heard it a thousand times, from family, from friends, from acquaintances, from neighbors, often with a disdainful tone in their voice, *Oh, he's weird, one of those health nuts who works out and eats right all the time, meditates and all that.*

This alone is a major obstacle and fear for many Americans when deciding to undertake a healthy lifestyle; the fear of not being accepted, of being called "weird," of taking time away from making money and acquiring all the nice things.

But take a step back and think for a minute. What good is it all if you are in a constant battle with your own body?...And *what,* please tell me, can be any more "weird" that this?… Quite frankly, constantly battling your own body because of YOUR OWN actions is pure stupidity! But, it is the status quo; the apathetic status quo of most Americans!

What was that advertisement some years ago that said, *When you've got your health, you've got just about everything!*? So true, because all the prestige, all the possessions, all the nice things, all the importance, and all the pomp and circumstance will not give you good health nor will they give you satisfaction when poor health knocks on your door.

As I approach 47, I have made image a "non-concern." As a result of my priorities, I have been blessed with a tremendous wealth in the ability to go most anywhere and do most anything I decide to undertake, physically or mentally, knowing my healthy body, mind, and spirit will see me through. That is an absolute *knowing* I possess.

Amazingly, since acquiring this *knowing,* required medical intervention has only occurred 4 times in my life: chicken pox, infected sweat gland, and 2 small benign skin cancer spots.

Not bad for a kid who grew up in a completely dysfunctional alcoholic home and who was an absolutely obese child until age 12, then had to work through the "garbage" from all of that for the next 12 years!

I can say with conviction that everyone *can* evolve to a higher level of health and well-being in all ways, despite any physical/mental/emotional limitations.

That being said, in answer to all those who expect to disintegrate and deteriorate and think that it's "normal to grow old and ill," I challenge you to change that thinking, change to action by utilizing the principles in this guide. Begin to ***KNOW*** your spirit never ages and that you can keep your body and mind from "growing old." Stop falling for all that other B.S. that many believe about aging.

Evolve! Break out of all that social conditioning and "enculturation!" Choose to live life to its fullest, to "keep on dancing," regardless of age!

So, go on, learn and practice what is in this guide and just watch that evolution of YOU take place…go forward and commit to changes for bettering your life, for the rest of your life! And, until we meet again for that "big dance in the sky," don't worry if "they" call you *"weird"*…we'll just keep on dancing… "they" won't be able to keep up! God Bless and God Speed on your most marvelous journey, *ever!*

12

"Health Care"

'Health,' with all that attacks it, both self-imposed and environmental, can become fragile. It can be reduced or obliterated in an instant. It has become an extremely *right now, this moment,* asset. It is our most important and precious asset.

But you and your body's ability and capability to defend against these attacks and, as well, to heal in the event of problems, is directly and singularly dependant upon your state-of-health *before* an unfortunate injury or illness strikes. This is the *true* meaning of "health care."

HealthCare, in today's society, has actually become a misnomer. It is, *in reality*, illness intervention, symptom suppression, and condition control and disease determination. This IS NOT health care. This is CRISIS CARE and LABELING OF CONDITIONS.

It is this type of approach to health care (crisis care and condition labeling) that has lead to the mess we're in today, both in personal health and in the system of care.

<u>Real</u> *health* **care** involves activities of daily living that encompass all of the aspects outlined in Part II, and *maintaining them as a lifestyle.* Anything less than this is less than healthy. Anything less than healthy is a life of illness intervention, symptom suppression, condition control…a life of crisis care.

Just look at most of the American population. They are *less than healthy* and spend a good deal of time in the battles of illness intervention, symptom suppression, and condition control. For the majority, their mindsets about their health have even "devolved" to the point where they wear their ailments, conditions, disabilities as "badges of prestige!" It has become "prestigious" to be ill!

The foregoing statistics come from groups of the most prominent physicians, human and exercise physiologists, psychologists, scientists, and spiritual leaders. The story they tell is shocking. *Based on the clinical and research data from these professional health institutions and organizations, the majority of Americans today, as a whole, are unhealthy and irresponsible in their lifestyles and thought patterns and activities of daily living.*

The majority of you reading this will *not* want to admit this truth but, inside, you **know** this truth.

I have had only one question in regard to it all…can this truth ever change?

Inside me, there has always been a knowing that it can. But inside me has also been a knowing that it will take harsh, hard measures; that most Americans will have to be forced to change. That day of forced change dawned on the 16th of April 2006 in the state of Massachusetts. *Mandatory Health Insurance* became a reality!

A Final Word

We have been so graciously and generously bestowed with a marvelous, miraculous perpetual motion machine, complete with an abundance of all things needed for its proper maintenance. Yet, that machine only has a "drive" gear. It allows us a one-way-only ride.

If we give it only the very best of all those things it needs to run all the way along that one-way ride, we shall experience that machine as marvelous and miraculous throughout the entire journey! A journey that will allow us to Live Healthy, Live Happy, Live Long…*LIVE* Life!

Namaste,

Dr. David Robinson

Quick Order Form

Please make check/MO to:

Infinity Publishing
1094 New DeHaven St.,
Suite 100,
West Conshohocken, PA 19428-2713

$12.95 per guide.

Please send the following number of guides _______

$12.95 X ______ guides = $_________

Please add $4.50 plus $1.00 per additional book for shipping and handling. Free Shipping on order of 20 or more.

Grand Total = $_________

Please print clearly

Name: ____

Address: ____

City: ____

State: ______________ Zip: ___________

CONCEIVE...

BELIEVE.....

ACHIEVE!

YOU SAY "IMPOSSIBLE"?

I SAY YOU CHANGE YOUR MIND TO… ***I'M****POSSIBLE!!…and just watch what happens!!!!*

From the deepest caverns of my heart,
From the farthest reaches of my soul,
To you!

Made in the USA
Monee, IL
08 November 2026

67380502R00059